The street cars of old St. John's

A Photo History

William Connors

Creative Publishers
P.O. Box 8660
St. John's, Newfoundland
1989

Appreciation is expressed to the *Canada Council* for publication assistance.

The Publisher acknowledges the contribution of the *Cultural Affairs Division of the Department of Municipal and Provincial Affairs, Government of Newfoundland and Labrador,* which has helped make this publication possible.

Printed in Canada by:
ROBINSON-BLACKMORE PRINTING AND PUBLISHING LTD.
P.O. Box 8660, St. John's, Newfoundland

Published by:
CREATIVE PUBLISHERS
A Division of Robinson-Blackmore Printing & Publishing Ltd.
P.O. Box 8660, St. John's, Newfoundland

Canadian Cataloguing in Publication Data
    Connors, William, 1925-
    The streetcars of old St. John's

    ISBN 0-920021-65-4

    1. St. John's Street Railway—History—Pictorial Works
    1. Title
    F727.S32C66   1989   388.4'6'09718
                                        C89-098619-3

This is a public service project of Newfoundland Light & Power Co. Limited.

Royalties will be donated to charity.

Cover hand coloured by Sylvia Cullum

Conductor Pat Parrell stands next to one of the original street cars during the early 1900's.

NLP Archives

Acknowledgements

I am indebted, as indeed are all his fellow citizens who are interested in preserving a record of a unique development in our heritage, to Dr. Angus Bruneau, President of Newfoundland Light & Power Co. Limited, who launched this project.

I wish to thank William Callahan, Managing Editor of The Evening Telegram, for permission to reprint news items from his paper and Gary L. Welland of the Toronto Dominion Bank for permission to use news items from The Daily News.

I am grateful for the assistance of the following people who enabled me to compile this publication. Mona Cram, David Leamon and Joan Grandy, Provincial Reference and Resource Library; Tony Murphy and Ann Devlin-Fischer, Provincial Archives; Catherine Murphy, St. John's Municipal Council; Jack Martin, Photographic Services, Memorial University of Newfoundland; Nancy Grenville, Centre for Newfoundland Studies Archives, Memorial University of Newfoundland; John Cardolis, American Legion Post 9; Dr. Martin Hogan, Newfoundland Transport Historical Society; Florence Drover, St. John's Transportation Commission; Edward Murphy, W. J. Murphy Limited; David Younker, Topsail Cinemas; Brendan Kenney, 10 Coronation Street, St. John's; William Garland, 315 Blackmarsh Road, St. John's; Clarence Noseworthy, 17 Roosevelt Avenue, Mount Pearl; Francis Rowe, 13 Winter Avenue, St. John's; Frank Walsh, Lawrence Ivany, John McGuire, Kay Aylward and Carol Taylor, Newfoundland Light & Power Co. Limited.

Foreword

It is more than four decades ago that the last street car followed the rails of Water Street into history. The changes that have taken place in St. John's and Newfoundland since that time have been many. Greater still has been the change since motor-man Michael Walsh and his fellow employees first took the cars to the streets in 1900.

In many ways the development of the city's street car system mirrored aspects of our lives today. Innovative and thorough engineering was required at the very beginning to build the Petty Harbour power plant, to lay the rails, and to construct what were then among the best-designed street cars anywhere. The sense of awe first experienced by the 30,000 residents of St. John's soon was replaced by dependence on the new means of transportation with the cars quickly becoming an accepted part of the city setting. Clearly the street cars met the needs of the citizens, and established a reputation for reliable, safe, and economical transportation, even under harsh weather conditions and increased wartime ridership. Meeting the changing needs of our customers with sound engineering and quality support systems continues today as part of the guiding mission of Newfoundland Light & Power.

This book combines scholarship with a nostalgic look back at St. John's during the first half of the 20th century. It is partly a response to the many questions and expressions of interest our Company regularly receives concerning the street cars. Their story is told by archival photographs combined with the words of the St. John's residents recorded in the newspapers of the time. In this way, the book recreates the period and, I am certain, will be of great interest for older readers whose memories may be stimulated, while realistically depicting the era for those of us who were not on hand.

I should like to congratulate William Connors and all others associated with the project which depended upon exhaustive research and the support of many over the past few years. On behalf of all who are part of Newfoundland Light & Power I should like to express our pride in the early employees of our Company who populate these pages, and in this retrospective look at their time.

Angus A. Bruneau
President and C.E.O.
Newfoundland Light & Power
Co. Limited

Introduction

The first electric public transit system in Canada was inaugurated in Windsor, Ontario in 1886. In all, 46 Canadian cities and suburbs adopted the electric street car. Halifax interests proposed forming a company, made up of St. John's businessmen, to operate a street railway in 1889, but final approval for the project was withheld in 1892 by the Newfoundland Legislature. It was not until 1900 that the St. John's Street Railway went into operation and, in common with many Canadian cities, it was fully integrated with an electric power company. Such a link was quite natural, especially in the early years when street car operations represented a major share of the power market.

The introduction of the street car system to St. John's happened as the town entered the twentieth century which would bring so many inventions and improvements that would change the way people lived. One newspaper in St. John's in 1900 described the wonder of the patrons of the street cars "as they enjoyed the strange sensation of being whirled along with such peculiar motive power." The speed of the original "Lariviere" street car was limited to 8 miles an hour and 4 miles an hour on curves. The "Birney" street cars were introduced in late 1925 and in 1937 the Municipal Council passed a motion to permit the speed of the street cars to be increased to 20 miles an hour.

The emergence of the automobile signalled the end of the golden age of the street car. Fixed to rails, they lacked the flexibility to go around obstacles. This proved to be a growing handicap as they had to share the streets with an increasing number of private cars. The war years put a great strain on the street car system in St. John's as the number of passengers increased from 1.5 million in 1940 to 2.9 million in 1944 with the influx of construction workers and American and Canadian servicemen.

The post-war years saw a street car system that was worn out, growing traffic congestion downtown and a demand for commuter service in an expanding St. John's. Another era in mass transit had already begun with the growing use of the motor bus and the street cars began to disappear across Canada. On September 15, 1948 the last street car made its final run in St. John's and returned to the car barn.

The habitual customer of the street car felt he was part of an informal club because of the social contacts it provided. He met people he did not encounter in the usual run of the day and the conversation, even with a stranger, was about politics, fishing or the vagaries of the weather. The fare was five cents and the cars were almost always on time. Every ten minutes one passed. The friendly conductor would hold the car for you if you were a little distance from the stop and signal you to slow down if he felt you were overdoing it. Come, let's journey back in time to the golden age of the street cars of old St. John's.

William Connors
St. John's, NF
September 15, 1989

Michael Walsh was employed as a motor-man on the street cars when they first appeared on the streets of St. John's on May 1st, 1900. When the operation of the street car system was discontinued, on September 15, 1948, he brought the last street car back to the car barn. This publication is dedicated to Michael Walsh and to all the employees of the street railway who served the citizens of St. John's, so well, for over forty-eight years.

When the St. John's Street Railway Bill was passed by the Newfoundland Legislature in 1896, approval of the bill was withheld by the Colonial Office at the insistence of Sir Francis Evans, the receiver of the bankrupt Newfoundland Railway Company. It was feared that the proposed street railway was an attempt to provide competition, on the Avalon Peninsula, to the Newfoundland Railway Company.

When the Newfoundland Government purchased the Newfoundland Railway Company, the passage of the St. John's Street Railway Bill was approved by the Colonial Office.

(Newfoundland) No. 73

Downing St.

20th Oct., '97

Sir, With reference to my dispatch, No. 6, of 28th of January last, respecting the St. John's Street Railway Bill, I have the honour to inform you that as the purchase of the Newfoundland Railway by the Colonial Government has been completed, I have advised Her Majesty to assent to this Bill, and I have now to transmit to you for the information of your Ministers, one sealed and six plain copies of the Order of Her Majesty in Council so declaring her assent.
I have, &c.,
J. Chamberlain

The Evening Herald
November 10, 1897

Governor

Sir. H.M. Murray K.C.B.

&c., &c., &c.

At the court at Balmoral, the 13th day of October, 1897. Present:- The Queeen's Most Excellent Majesty, His Royal Highness Prince Christian, Lord James of Hereford, Sir Fleetwood Edwards.

Whereas - On the 8th day of September, 1896 the Governor of the colony of Newfoundland reserved a Bill passed by the Legislative Council and the House of Assembly of the said Colony, entitled "An Act to incorporate the St. John's Street Railway Company, and for other purposes," for the signification of Her Majesty's pleasure thereon: And Whereas - The said Bill so reserved as aforesaid has been before Her Majesty in Council, and it is expedient that the said Bill should be assented by Her Majesty: Now, therefore Her Majesty doth by this present Order, by and with the advice of Her Majesty's Privy Council, declare her assent to the said bill.

C. L. Peel

The Evening Herald
November 10, 1897

The Railway Deal

. . . He is to build an electrical railway in St. John's, and pave Water Street for the sum of $140,000.

The Government agrees upon construction of the Street railway, to procure the paving of Water Street with granite blocks. The work to be carried out by the Contractor under and according to the specifications to be provided for which the Government agrees to pay the sum of $140,000.

The Government agrees to grant him the exclusive use of Petty Harbour Pond, or Petty Harbour Long Pond, or such other lake in the vicinity of St. John's, as he may select for the purpose of providing power for his Electric Railway. In the event of selecting Long Pond, he undertakes to construct at his own cost a sufficient water main to and near the West End terminus, the use of which shall be at the disposal of the St. John's Fire Department when necessary in case of fire.

The Evening Herald
February 22, 1898

MUN Photography

Sir Robert Reid

Robert Gillespie Reid was born in Scotland in 1842 and was a distinguished bridge builder and railway contractor when he obtained an important railway contract in 1890 from the Newfoundland Government. He transferred his operations to Newfoundland and besides his activities in transportation and communications, he built the first hydro electric development, for public use, in Newfoundland at Petty Harbour. Electricity from this station was first transmitted to St. John's on April 19, 1900 by the St. John's Street Railway Company which became part of the operations of the Reid Newfoundland Company.

The St. John's Street Railway purchased the St. John's Electric Light Company. The Petty Harbour Plant then provided electricity not only for the street car system but also for the homes and businesses of St. John's.

This great builder was knighted in 1907 and died in Montreal in 1908. He was succeeded as President by his son, William (afterwards Sir William). Two other sons were directors of the company, Harry and Robert, Jr.

The Petty Harbour Works

The electric power plant at Petty Harbour is being well advanced. The power house when completed will be 15 feet high, and already one side and end are finished except about 2 feet from the top, while all the windows in the ends so far put up are complete. The walls are built of whinstone and are 3 feet thick. The remaining side and end are not yet begun as men are engaged excavating for the solid foundation. It will be an enormous job to get the heavy iron conducting pipe in position. It is 8 feet in diameter, while a small one of 4 feet in diameter will also feed from the main. The pipe is 75 feet high and one can imagine the force with which the water fills this will fall. A sledge driven with force against it would rebound, and the heaviest shot would not penetrate this rush of confined water. The waste water from the "turbine" will lead to the sea over a new river bed or "tail race," and promises to be of service to the people. The work is being rushed along but it will be yet some time ere everything is complete. The place is now well worth a visit.

The Evening Herald
November 23, 1899

Petty Harbour Hydro Electric Plant, 1900. A wooden flume 3,300 feet in length, 8 feet square inside, open on top, and made from 500,000 feet of timber ran along the side of the steep hill and disappeared into a tunnel which was blasted through the solid rock of Gull Hill for a distance of 350 feet. The water carried through the flume then dropped 180 feet through a 6 feet in diameter steel pipe to power the electric generators in the plant.

NLP Archives

The Generators

We understand that Mr. Reid has contracted with John Starr, Son & Co. of Halifax, agents in the Maritime Provinces for the Westinghouse Electric Co. for the electrical equipment of the street railway. The electrical generators at the station will be equal to 1,500 horse power, and these and other apparatus will be made by Westinghouse Electric and Manufacturing Co. of Pittsburg for whom Messrs. Starr are agents. This is the same firm that equipped the original Electric Light Station in St. John's and renewed the same after its entire destruction by fire.

The Evening Herald
April 26, 1899

Interior of Petty Harbour plant, 1900. Shown left to right, Frank Wing, Jack Halley and William Howlett. Mr. Wing was the first person to be electrocuted in Newfoundland when he received a charge of 15,000 volts on April 11, 1901 and died instantly. Mr. Howlett was killed in 1911 when a board he was holding came into contact with the revolving armature of one of the generators. Both accidents occurred in the Petty Harbour plant. Mr. Halley joined the St. John's Electric Light Company, a predecessor company, in 1885 and retired from the old Newfoundland Light and Power Company in 1943.

Laying the Rails

Last evening the first rails were laid on Water Street on wooden ties. The track evidently will be a double one, and hundreds viewed it exhibiting much curiosity. Each day the scene there is most remarkable. A large gang of lusty fellows wield the picks with the dexterity for which Newfoundland navvies are famed, and a large section of the street has been cut down to the required level. Mr. Burton is well liked by his men and is rushing matters. It is outrageous, however, not to have gangways across the curbs where bye-ways intervene, and last night several citizens escaped narrowly from sustaining broken limbs or necks. The watchman employed cannot be everywhere and the sooner this matter is remedied the better.

The Evening Herald
August 9, 1899

Laying the tracks on Water Street for the Street Railway, 1899. Besides paving Water Street with granite blocks, the Reids also had to construct concrete sidewalks and gutters on both sides of the street.

The First Street Car

The first of the street railway cars arrived in town by yesterday's local train, and is a magnificent article. It was built by A.C. Lariviere, the famous street car constructor of Montreal, but is superior to any he has ever put out of hand. This is one of the finest cars of the kind ever constructed and is a foot longer than those of Montreal city, for Mr. W.D. Reid, having taken special care in the construction, noticed a defect in the Canadian cars that he remedied in these. The interior of the car is magnificent, being upholstered in light green plush with spring cushions running along either side, and with straps held in position by brass rods for passengers standing, so that it can easily contain 50 people. An enclosure for the motor man is at either end. The windows are on a swivel and swing from the centre, while electric lights, two incandescent lamps at either end and four in the centre will give all the illumination needed at night. The doors are automatic and swing back on the opening of one. The car is built of oak and ash, with handsome panelling, and those who have ridden on street cars claim these to be superior to any they have ever seen. It is now at the railway station yard side tracked, awaiting final fitting.

The Evening Herald
August 24, 1899

Newfoundland Railway terminus at Fort William. The crowd is believed to be assembled for the laying of the corner stone of the Avalon Hotel, site of the present Hotel Newfoundland, on March 20, 1900. The Avalon Hotel was never built. Note the arc lamp in the foreground and a street car, (probably the first one), in the background, to the right. The building with the oval roof is the Prince's Rink which was destroyed by fire in 1941.

Street Cars Run for the First Time

For the first time two electric street cars started from Fort William at 12:45 today, and in charge of Engineer W. McKay, came slowly along Ordnance Street and up Duckworth Street as far as Holloway Street where the rails run into Water Street. A large crowd of people were attracted to the novel sight. A few passengers were in the cars, amongst whom were Messrs. W.D. and R.G. Reid. At one o'clock the rail was cleared and made ready on Holloway Street, and the cars came down into Water Street, where, although it was dinner hour, a large crowd remained on the ground. After a little delay on Water Street, during which the car behind was filled up with passengers, both cars moved up Water Street with a good degree of speed, the sidewalks being lined with people all the way uptown.

The Evening Telegram
May 1, 1900

The inaugural run of the St. John's Street Railway, May 1, 1900. The original street cars were manufactured by the Lariviere Car Company of Montreal. The open space in the background is where the War Memorial is located.

Free rides

Yesterday the street cars were put in motion for the first time, and attracted a large number of curious onlookers. Two cars were run up Water Street, the first containing Mr. W.D. Reid, Hon. Dr. Skelton, Dr. Pilot and representatives of the press, and other prominent citizens. The cars ran smoothly, and throughout the day were patronized by crowds of people, who enjoyed alike the novelty and the free ride. It was thought the cars would be the cause of frightening horses, but this did not appear to any extent, and no accident is reported for the day. As soon as the rails are made ready, and the service regularly started, it will be found of much value and duly appreciated by citizens generally.

The Daily News
May 2, 1900

Free rides, May 1, 1900. The street cars are shown on Water Street East at the foot of Holloway Street.

As far as Torphy's

The street cars ran up as far as Victoria Park yesterday afternoon, and Mr. P. Redmond hoisted the Union Jack on the Park flagstaff in honour of the event. Men were engaged at clearing the rails as far as Torphy's where the cars will likely run today.

The Daily News
May 4, 1900

Street car at the Crossroads, Water Street West during the early 1900's. Torphy's public house is shown in the background. The cars were manned by two men, a motorman and a conductor, and two seats ran the length of the car facing one another. The cars were yellow in colour and had wooden bodies. Note the cow catcher in front of the street car.

NLP Archives

Breaking in the horses

Last evening the electric cars did splendid work, being on time at the east and the west terminals. People of all classes crowded them, seats were at a premium and the conductors had to push their way thro, in collecting fares, the crowd holding the straps, so difficult was it to obtain runs. On the paved section of Water St., to 'break in' horses or to familiarize them with passing at any time the ponderous looking coaches, men were riding steeds bare-backed, charging them against the incoming cars or, backing on the sidewalks, sped after them to accustom them to the sight. Animals attached to vehicles of every size and description from the handsome turn out of the merchant or medico to the dray of the teamster or box cart of the coat vendor, were kept well in check at the corners of side streets, up which the frightened steeds scampered. Along by Messrs. Allan's, Walsh's, McCarthy's. Healey's and other stores, ponies jumped on the sidewalk and were only grasped in time by onlookers, while their owners rushed from these stores to secure them. During the night the cars, which, being illuminated, looked very handsome, were packed with people as they rushed up and down Water St., and did not cease running until 11 p.m. We would advise the necessity of the checking of the speed at street crossings and of keeping youngsters from hanging to the cars while in motion.

The Evening Telegram
May 3, 1900

Two street cars going west on the south track on Water Street during the early 1900's. The other street car is turning east into Water Street from Adelaide Street on the Belt Line. The use of the south track was later discontinued.

And the band played on

On Thursday night after the parade was over, W.D. Reid, Esq., with his usual kindness put one of the street cars at the disposal of the Inspector General, when the Police Band with a few other guests, including representatives of the Herald and the News got on board and rode around town till midnight. The band played lively airs all the time.

The Daily News
June 2, 1900

St. John's Street Railway employees, circa 1900. The name of the company was changed to the Reid Newfoundland Company in 1901 and the street cars were identified with the new name. The flags on the street cars indicate the celebration of a special event. The news item on the opposite page refers to the celebrations that took place in St. John's, after the fall of Pretoria, during the Boer War.

St. John's Transportation Commission

Demon rum

What would have been another street car tragedy was only averted on Saturday night last, by the quick-sightedness of a motor man. As one of the cars was going down Holloway Street, two men were seen lying across the track, and the car was brought to a stop, not, however, before the fender came into contact with one of the men, both of whom were discovered to be drunk and insensible to their danger. As the same car was proceeding up Adelaide Street shortly afterwards, another drunken fellow rolled up against it and the conductor had to jump off the thrust him out of danger. Both of these occurrences might have resulted in serious accidents, and the conductor and motor man held responsible for them, when they were in no way to blame. Adelaide and Holloway Streets are the worst parts of the street car line, and it would be as well that the policemen on these beats keep an extra look out for the future.

The Daily News
May 27, 1901

Street cars turning into Holloway Street from Duckworth Street during the early 1900's.

Street car schedule

In another column will be found a time table for the running of the street car system which will be found useful to the large number of patrons. We wish to direct attention to a new idea which will be convenient viz., the notice of stopping places along the entire route. Passengers will find at convenient distances, a notice which reads 'cars stop here' and it will be to their advantage to congregate at these centres and thus avoid delay or danger.

Daily News
July 19, 1901

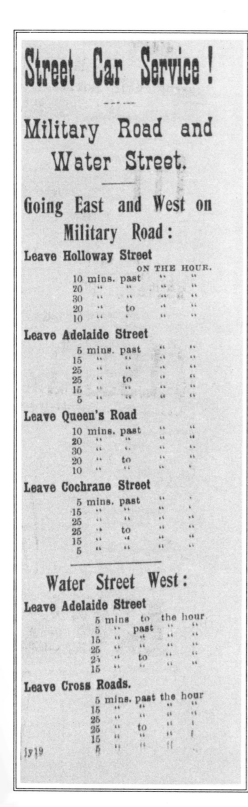

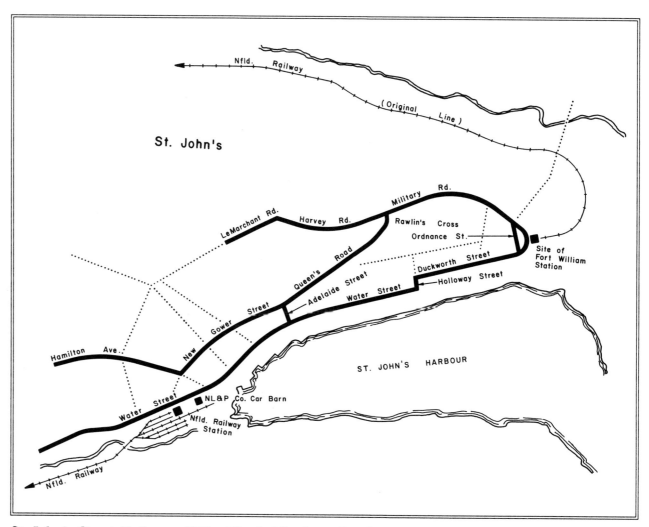

St. John's Street Railway, 1900. The LeMarchant Road and New Gower Street spur lines were discontinued in 1902. The original line used Ordnance Street but when new rails were laid in 1925, the line was moved to run in front of the Newfoundland Hotel which was under construction.

An engineering report dated 1922 described the street car route as commencing at the Crossroads, Water Street West, along Water Street, up Holloway Street, east on Duckworth Street, up Military Road and then by Queen's Road to the foot of Adelaide Street. From there the street cars returned by the same route to the west end of Water Street.

The Daily News
July 19, 1901

Drafting Dept., NLP

Owing to the dust

The street cars were held up until noon yesterday from some disarrangement of machinery. In the afternoon owing to the dust, they were well patronized.

The Evening Herald
July 1, 1901

Street cars at the junction of Adelaide Street and Water Street. The section of Water Street shown escaped the great fire of 1892, so that architecturally it is a good example of the whole of old Water Street since the fire of 1846 which destroyed most of downtown St. John's.

We have moved

The Reid Co.'s street car express and ticket offices will be located on the street flat of the Gazette building. In future, all other departments going to the new west end station.

The Evening Herald
January 12, 1903

Street car No. 6 amid the celebrations on the occasion of the visit of the Duke and Duchess of Cornwall and York, 1901. Building on the right was Ayre's Department Store, site of Atlantic Place, and the building partially shown on the left was the Gazette Building, later known as the Bank of Montreal.

The sprinkler

All yesterday the Reid Company had employees fitting up the new sprinkling car at the Municipal Basin. The large circular tank which will be placed on the car has a capacity of 2000 gallons of water, and it will be driven by electricity over the street railway system, going when necessity requires it, at greater speed than the average tram car. It will throw copious jets of water from both sides and the rear of the car, and now that the warm weather is with us will do good work keeping the streets free of dust. It will begin work tomorrow.

Evening Herald
July 14, 1903

Electrically driven sprinkler travelling east on Queen's Road. Note the jets of water on each side of the sprinkler which kept down the dust. The B.I.S. Hall is in the background and the building on the right is the Gower Street Church. This picture was reproduced from a 35 mm movie film, circa 1910.

Keep cool

Something went wrong in a street car bound up Theatre Hill yesterday afternoon and it slid back 3 or 4 feet. The motorman quickly had his brakes on, stopping the car, but two lady passengers were stampeded and one jumped through the doorway. Even if the car did go down the grade, the brakes would of checked her speed and in cases of this kind, people should keep cool and refrain from endangering their lives by jumping when there is no necessity to do so.

The Evening Herald
October 2, 1903

Street car stopped in front of what is now known as the Cathedral Parish Hall on Queen's Road during the early 1900's. This building was built in 1893 and the tower was removed in 1932. Bishop Spencer College was located there until 1919 and the Model School occupied the ground floor until the early 1960's. The open space in the foregound is now occupied on the left by a municipal park and on the right by the Sergeant's Memorial.

Francis Rowe

No delay

The sweeper with Inspector Andrews in charge during the storm of last night made several circuits of the left line and the Water Street car tracks keeping the rails free of snow so that the cars ran till midnight without the least delay.

The Evening Herald
January 4, 1904

Street car, Water Street West in the vicinity of the Railway Station in 1904. A second street car and an A-frame shed for doing minor repairs on the street cars, are visible in the centre background. To enable workmen to service the cars, a pit was dug similar to a garage grease pit. The pit reached below sea level, and at high tide the men had to work with mud and water up to their knees.

St. John's Municipal Council

Keeping the line open

The street cars have had hard work to keep the line open today. Time again they were stuck, owing to the drift, though the sweepers were kept constantly on the move. Ice forms rapidly on the rails and even flangers cannot keep it clear. A small army of men are employed by the Company all over the line in their efforts to keep the service going.

The Evening Herald
January 20, 1904

Clearing the tracks on Duckworth Street at the intersection with Cochrane Street 1904. Man with the astrakhan hat is Mayor George Shea, the first elected mayor of St. John's, and next to him is City Engineer, John Ryan.

Using the sidewalks

Yesterday afternoon the Reid Company had a gang of men throwing back the snow along the belt line. It was piled high by the sweeper and on Military Road there is no place for truckmen or sleighs to get along except on the sidewalk, and danger exists to those leaving their homes, especially children.

The Evening Herald
December 20, 1904

Looking west on Military Road, 1904. The snow was often piled so high on each side of the track, the horse drawn sleighs had to use the sidewalks. Note where the sleighs crossed the tracks to get to King's Bridge Road.

Shortage of water

The lack of electricity for want of motive power and light, inconvenienced many the past two nights. Saturday night was the worst experienced in the city for some time, as several business places had to close up for want of light. All the moving picture shows opened but suddenly they were placed in total darkness. A panic was expected but the emergency had been expected by the managers and instantly all the doors were flung open by the ushers. Practically the same circumstances existed on Water St. where many of the stores had only electric lights installed, they finding it very difficult to locate the customer's desires by candle light; eventually several closed before the scheduled hour. Those who were fortunate enough in having gas, were not inconvenienced in any way. Not only were the shops without light, but the streets were pitched into total darkness.

All this was due to the shortage of water at Petty Harbour the quantity coming through the flume being not sufficient to supply the town with the necessary light or motor power for any definite period. When the shore train arrived the station was thronged and passengers had some difficulty getting out. Only a few lanterns were on hand, not nearly sufficient for the purpose. The street cars were off and darkness was supreme.

The Evening Herald
August 24, 1908

Street car stopped at the intersection of Granny Bates Hill and Theatre Hill (Queen's Road). Holloway's Photographic Studio is shown, on the right, at the foot of Henry Street. The conductor and the motor man are stood outside the street car observing a political rally. Circa 1909.

Winter works

The matter of snow clearing where the street railway runs has not yet been decided upon. The Reid Co. have several horses and a number of men along Water Street this morning removing some of the snow piled up by the sweeper. The Council also have their horses and men engaged removing the snow at the junctions of Cross streets and also from the entrances to the coves. The Employment Bureau also sent a few men who were in urgent need of work to remove the snow from the South side of Water Street. The Bureau is hoping to make arrangements with the Reid Co. to employ a number of men clearing the street railway track, and it is expected that some men will be sent to work this evening. The street car service along Water Street is at present only using the track on the North side.

The Evening Telegram
January 20, 1922

Clearing the tracks on Water Street West. Note the sweeper in the background. The buildings in the background were demolished to build the naval facilities used during World War II. Circa 1920.

Melba

Malcolm McEachern, the eminent Scotch basso, who comes from the Strand Theatre, Broadway, New York, makes his debut at the Nickel Theatre today. Mr. McEachern is an artist with a world wide reputation and has toured two years with the prima donna, Melba, who has spoken and written very highly of him. He has a wonderful selection of songs and he is sure to please and charm our people. He will sing each afternoon at 4, and twice in the evenings. A very fine picture programme has been arranged for today.

The Evening Herald
July 26, 1920

Street car No. 1 is shown passing the foot of Prescott Street going west on Water Street during the summer of 1920. Note the sign on the front of the street car promoting a concert at the Nickel Theatre.

Provincial Reference Library

The St. John's Light and Power Company

During the past few days three new companies have been incorporated under the Companies Act which will interest the public greatly. They are the St. John's Light and Power Company Ltd., the Newfoundland Dockyards Limited and the Mines and Forests Limited (Newfoundland).

The incorporators of all three companies are Harry Duff Reid, Robert Gillespie Reid and Charles O'Neill Conroy.

The St. John's Light and Power Company has an authorized capital of $1,500,000 and its purpose is to supply electricity for all purposes for which it may be used, to carry on any kind of manufacturing or trade, and do any other business which may be carried out in connection therewith.

The Evening Herald
December 15, 1920

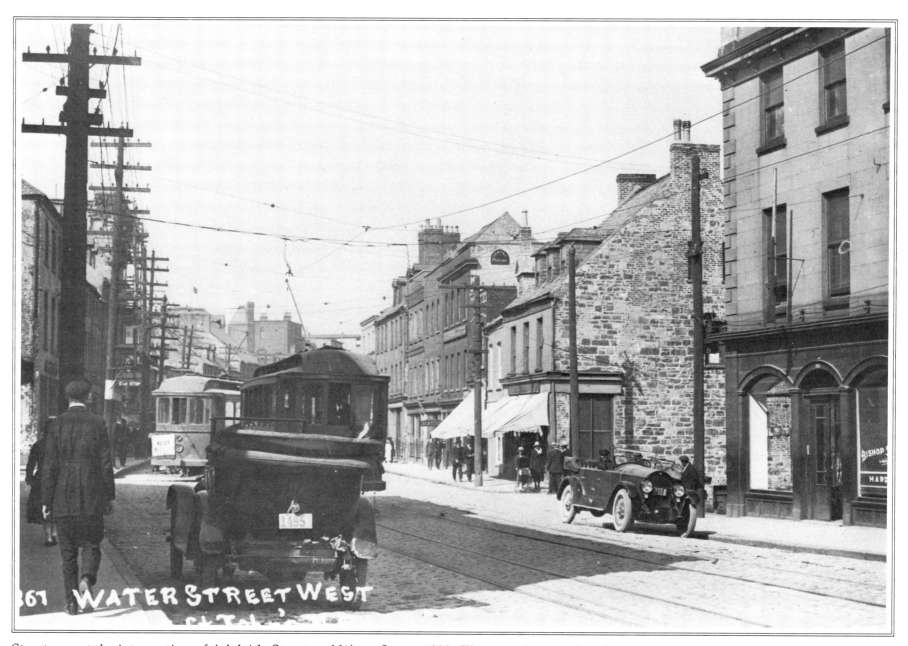

Street cars at the intersection of Adelaide Street and Water Street, 1920. This was the year that the street railway and the electrical distribution business were separated from other interests of the Reid Newfoundland Company to form the St. John's Light and Power Company.

Blocking the line

A truck driver who was obstructing the street car service was fined costs. According the to evidence, he left his car overhanging the car track on Military Road and went into a store. The driver of the street car rang the bell and eventually had to go to the store to get the truck removed. The driver, instead of hurrying to remove the truck, gave the conductor a lot of abuse.

The Evening Telegram
March 1, 1937

Lariviere street car coming down Military Road during the early 1920's. The monument shown on the right was erected in 1920 in memory of Ethel Dickenson, who gave her life nursing victims of the Spanish Flu epidemic in St. John's in 1918. The monument was later moved to the park in front of present Hotel Newfoundland.

Dr. Martin Hogan

Unused rails

At City Hall

In the matter of the unused street car rails, west of Rawlins Cross on Military Road, Superintendent Morris stated that the question as to whether these would be used in the future was at present in abeyance, but if the Council would defer the matter at least another fortnight, pending instructions from Head Office, it would then be given consideration. As to the condition of rails in other parts of the town, he stated they would receive immediate attention.

The Daily News
May 1, 1925

One of the original street cars at Rawlins Cross during the early 1920's. Leo O'Mara's drug store was on the corner and next to it the 'Blue Puttee' which was a popular spot with the younger set. A spur line ran up Military Road from Rawlins Cross in 1900 but was discontinued in 1902. It was proposed in 1929 to extend the line across LeMarchant Road from Rawlins Cross but the proposal was abandoned when Council refused approval to raise the fare from 5 to 7 cents.

Edward Murphy

Killam takes over

In connection with the recently formed Newfoundland Light and Power Company, we learn that three local directors have been added to the Board. They are Sir M.G. Winter, Messrs. W.S. Monroe and C.A.C. Bruce. The Company is controlled by the Royal Securities Co., of which Mr. I.W. Killam is President, and is under the supervision of the Montreal Engineering Company, which is a subsidiary of the Royal Securities. The Montreal Engineering Company have been closely associated with many public utility enterprises, chief among which may be mentioned the Camagney Electric Company of Cuba, the Calgary Electric, the Western Power of Canada, the Ottawa Electric, and the Nova Scotia Light, Heat and Power. It is hoped that in a short time operations will be begun to give to St. John's and the vicinity a service which will be thoroughly efficient, and that a complete revision of the schedule of charges for power will be made. It may be added that it will be upon the latter that public attention will be chiefly focused. In order to encourage public interest in the enterprise bonds will be placed on the local market, further information in connection with which will be given at an early date.

The Evening Telegram
February 28, 1924

Izaak Walton Killam

Izaak Walton Killam was born in Nova Scotia in 1885 and was a protege of Max Aitken (later Lord Beaverbrook) the founder of Royal Securities. When Aitken left for London to pursue a career in journalism and politics, Killam purchased Royal Securities which became the most important finance house in Canada. Killam went on to own electric utilities and tramway companies in Mexico, South America and the Caribbean besides electric utilities and pulp mills across Canada.

In 1924 he purchased the assets of the St. John's Light & Power Company, a Reid Company which operated the street railway in St. John's, incorporated Newfoundland Light and Power Company Ltd. and made it part of International Power. Just before Newfoundland joined Canada in 1949, Killam took Newfoundland Light and Power out of the orbit of International Power and sold his shares to the public.

Killam died in 1956 and his personal fortune was used to establish scholarships and foundations for advanced study and research.

Upgrading Petty Harbour plant

The extensive improvements which have been in progress the last few months at the Petty Harbour Power House will be completed early in the new year. Mr. Crocutt, of the Armstrong, Whitworth Company of England, is now on the spot installing the new turbine. Excellent progress is being made by the W.I. Bishop Company in the construction of the big dam and it will be finished about the end of January.

The Daily News
December 17, 1926

POWER HOUSE AND NEW FLUME UNDER CONSTRUCTION AT PETTY HR. N.F.

Newfoundland Light and Power Company Limited commenced the reconstruction of the Petty Harbour plant in 1926 and the project was completed in a little over a year. The power house was extended 30 feet, the height of the building was increased by 10 feet and new generating equipment installed. A new woodstave pipe 3200 feet in length was built and major work was carried out on the water storage system. St. John's, which had to do without electricity during times of drought, now had a dependable supply of power.

Provincial Archives

Be sure

Every time you ride in a street car you take a chance. Ring Percie Johnson & Son about that accident policy now.

The Daily News
May 1, 1925

A group of Boy Scouts size up the operation of getting street car No. 3 back on the tracks. The derailment took place on the eastern section of Military Road in 1924 or 1925. Note that one car is identified as Reid Newfoundland Company and the other, Newfoundland Light & Power Company.

VALEDICTION

To the Old Street Cars of St. John's on the Point of Retirement.

Farewell, ye iron servants one and all,
At last ye've heard well earned retirement's call.
No more thy welcome comings shall we greet,
Or restful, journey home upon thy seats.

Ah, we who love ye well night three decades,
And watched ye grow to youth, from youth to age.
Our children's playmates, our own honest friends,
Are sad to see our long acquaintance end.

Come shed a tear, ye that have tears to shed,
For ancient friends, the wheels of whom are sped.
Remember not their wee eccentric ways,
Allow them all, the peace of waning days.

For ever hoary age must give to youth
The right of way, and liberty forsooth;
And passing leave them in their place behind,
To earn the name and worth which they resigned.

And if the new who come to take the place,
Of those who, finis to their life must trace;
Shall prove but half as worthy as the last,
They shall do ample honour to the past.

Nemo Dixit

The Evening Telegram
November 4, 1925

66

Employees of the street railway in their navy blue uniforms. When Newfoundland Light and Power Company Limited was incorporated in 1924 and brought in new street cars in late 1925 the colour of the uniforms was changed to gray.

The new cars arrive

Last night six of the new street cars were hauled from Shea's wharf to
Water Street. A temporary track was laid from the wharf to Water Street
as far up as where the old track is in the street, just opposite the Custom
House. From here the cars where brought up to the foot of Holloway
Street and will be placed on the regular rails to be taken to the car shop
and put in readiness to go in the service. The work of bringing them to
Water Street was accomplished in an efficient manner.

The Daily News
November 7, 1925

One of the new street cars that went into service in late 1925 is shown in front of the new car barn which was built by Newfoundland Light and Power Company when it purchased the street railway from the Reid interests in 1924. The new street cars were operated by one man instead of two, as on the original cars, and were manufactured by the Birney Car Company of Ottawa. The cars were red in colour with all steel bodies.

NLP Archives

The sweeper

The street sweeper created quite a furor amongst the houses as it sped up and down Water Street today. A cloud of drift is thrown from it to the sidewalk, enveloping everything. Pedestrians caught in the shower emerged covered with snow driven into their clothing. Horses had to be held firmly, fearing they would bolt as the car passed.

The Evening Herald
December 19, 1903

Included with the new equipment brought in by Newfoundland Light and Power Company was a 150 horsepower sweeper. It did an excellent job in keeping the lines open during the worst winter storms.

Ear-splitting racket

The street cars make an ear-splitting racket when turning curves, at Rawlin's Cross, and perhaps elsewhere—that it incontrovertible. Those who live in the vicinity must have the sweetest tempers, with midnight as their time of retiring, and 8:00 a.m. as the rising hour, unless, of course, they prefer meditation to sleep. Surely it is possible in some manner to lessen the nerve-wrecking ordeal to which the aged, the infirm and the nerve-racked are subjected.

In every other respect the Street Car Service is praiseworthy. It is remarkable how quickly the public has adapted itself to the one man system, and how generally it is preferred. Much of its popularity is due directly to the courtesy, and efficiency of the driver-conductors. The speed, if not as great as in the first days of the new service, is all that is required or desired. The cars run well on time, and the service is as reliable as may be reasonably expected. General Manager Morris has done excellent work and is seeing results.

The Daily News
August 2, 1926

Inspector Pat Parrell stands beside street car No. 10 at the foot of Adelaide Street, circa 1926. When the new street cars went into operation, the firm of Gerald S. Doyle was the first company to use the ends of all seven street cars, then in use, to advertise its products. The building on the left was occupied by the Broadway House of Fashion, which was destroyed by fire in 1931, when five buildings were gutted in the worst fire in St. John's in twenty-three years.

How sweet it is

At noon today a street car struck a puncheon of molasses at the foot of Holloway Street bursting the head and completely covering the truck-man with the contents of the package. There will be evidently a demand for damages by the owner of the sweet stuff.

The Evening Herald
December 12, 1904

July 1st parade to the National War Memorial during the late 1920's. The parade detoured around a street car on Water Street at the street railway siding between Prescott Street and Holloway Street.

Trolley runs wild

At 3 p.m. yesterday when the air-brake on street car number 15, in charge of operator Molloy, failed to hold, the car ran wild over Theatre Hill, jumped the curve at Adelaide Street and only came to a stop sixty yards further on after smashing the front of some houses on the lower side of the street. Six passengers were in the car and one man jumped from the back window. No one was hurt of those remaining in the car, and the man who jumped, beyond a shaking up, was not injured.

The car cut off two electric light poles on the south side of the street, tore the front out of two houses and then stopped, still upright, about two feet from another house.

The Daily News
July 25, 1927

Street car No. 15 is shown finally stopped in front of a house, now known as Gosse's Lounge on New Gower Street, opposite the present City Hall. The accident happened July 24, 1927, as the street car ran wild down Theatre Hill (Queen's Road) and jumped the tracks on the curve turning into Adelaide Street and did considerable damage as it proceeded up New Gower Street.

Brendan Kenney

Tracks are dangerous

The street car tracks are reported to be several inches above the surface in places and dangerous to traffic and pedestrians. Arrangements will have to be made to have the tracks filled in with clay in the places most needed.

The Evening Telegram
April 5, 1929

Street car No. 12 at the Crossroads, Water Street West during the late 1920's. The West End Post Office was located in the third house from Kent's store. Note the styles on the two ladies crossing the street and the beach rocks used for drains.

Provincial Archives

Record of progress

The Newfoundland Light and Power Company which took over the street railway and lighting system in St. John's in 1924, has done much to improve conditions since then. One of its first works was the reconstruction of the street railway, and new equipment throughout. New concrete car barns and offices were built. The whole street railway was relaid in 1925 with new 70 pound 'T' rails and eight new steel, one-man cars of the latest type were imported, replacing the old, worn out cars then in use; and a new 150 horsepower sweeper imported for snow clearing. Since the new equipment was installed on the street railway it has been maintained in continuous operation summer and winter, and even the heaviest snow falls have failed to interrupt the service.

The Daily News
December 31, 1930

Street car going east on Military Road, 1930. Building on the right was Field Hall, a boarding school for boys attending Bishop Field College. This building was torn down in 1933. The building in the background was Canon Wood Hall which was demolished after a major fire in 1966. St. Thomas Church is on the right.

Dr. Martin Hogan

From the boys

At noon on New Year's Eve, the general office of the L & Power Co. Ltd. was the scene of a happy gathering when they took advantage of the closing of the old year to collectively express their esteem and affection to their manager, Mr. W.J. Morris, which took the form of a presentation of a handsome lacquered Japanese coffee table, the inscription on the silver plate reading:

From 'The Boys' of the Nfld. L & Power Co. Ltd., to the Manager, J.W. Morris, M.B.E., Dec., 1901-1936.

The Hon. Nathan Andrews made the presentation which he did very fittingly and in doing so handed the recipient a greeting album in which were autographs of every local employee of the Company.

The Evening Telegram
January 12, 1937

Employees Street Railway, July 1936

Standing, left to right—M. Walsh(Track Foreman), D. Walsh, M. Morgan, C. Noseworthy, H. Healey, T. Morgan(Barn Foreman), Mrs. Brewer, Miss Chafe, S. Short, W.R. Bishop, R.J. Moore, Hon. N. Andrews(Supt.), L. Walsh, F. Noel, W. Dawe (Insp.), J. Short, W.G. Morgan, R. Mercer, W. McKay, A. Strange, H. Noseworthy.

Sitting, left to right—P.H. Tucker, E. Walker, H. Bartlett, R.A. Joy, P. Parrell(Insp.)

Travelling billboards

Probably one of the most striking and effective measures being employed by the Anti-T.B. campaigners in their efforts to sell Christmas Seals for the battle against tuberculosis, is that featured on the local street cars.

As they go rolling around the city, the large white painted letters on the sides 'BUY T.B. CHRISTMAS SEALS', accompanied by the double-barred cross, the symbol of anti-t.b., create a continual reminder to thousands that an active campaign, the first of its kind in the country, is now in operation to stamp out tuberculosis in Newfoundland.

The Daily News
November 27, 1944

The street cars were used to promote the sale of Christmas Seals in 1944. During the early years of the Second World War, the street cars carried patriotic slogans such as 'Grow a Victory Garden' and 'Buy War Savings Certificates.'

Tying it together

The street-car system was held up for a few minutes yesterday afternoon when a west bound car on Water Street broke down. The conductor was forced to evacuate the car, and many pedestrians watched, with mixed emotions, him doing his very best to tie some section of the under-carriage together with the aid of a coil of material which looked very much like rope, while he stood ankle deep in a puddle of water.

The Daily News
March 7, 1945

Derailments were not an uncommon occurrence on the street railway system. Street car No. 11 is shown being towed back on the tracks having been derailed on Water Street West during the war years. The side of the street car carried the slogan 'Buy War Bonds and Stamps.'

THERE'S PLENTY OF ROOM AT THE REAR

When I was young and in my prime
I heard the old folks say—
There's plenty of room at the top, my lad,
You should strive for it, day by day,
But now a change, the tune we hear
On the street car, morn and night,
Is step back, step back and make more space
There's lots of room at the rear.

I'm rickety now, with pains in my legs
From standing, whilst driving down town,
I'm very polite, more so, than at home
For I jump, to let ladies sit down,
I'm weak, and all in, a bit dizzy am I
From hearing a voice ringing clear,
"Ladies and Gentlemen—will you please move back,
There's plenty of room at the rear."

Conductors on street cars, are wonderful men,
With patience, and tack, in galore,
'Tis marvellous how they manage to stow
Two hundred, with space for a score
But when we are jammed, like sardines in a can,.
'Tis only a saint who won't swear,
When we hear the conductor's melodious voice
"Folks—there's plenty of room at the rear."

Tim Shannahan
The Daily News
February 13, 1943

Street car in front of the Railway Station during the war years. Because of blackout regulations, the fenders of the motor cars were painted white and head lights were partially covered. The street car in the background is in front of the former offices and car barn of the Newfoundland Light and Power Company.

A new route

The work of re-railing the street car system is progressing rapidly in the east end of the city and has now been completed as far as Wood Street. In this section a new route is being taken. Where formerly the cars came down Ordnance Street and around the East End Fire Hall, they will now run along the road on the upper side of the park, there crossing in front of the main entrance to the new hotel.

The Daily News
August 28, 1925

Street car No. 17 in front of the old Newfoundland Hotel. The street car line originally ran down Ordnance Street but was changed to run in front of the new hotel which was opened in 1926. Circa 1945.

Changing the rule of the road

After twelve hours of driving to the right, at noon today, St. John's could be said to have taken to the new driving rule of the road, which was ushered in at the stroke of midnight, like the royal swans took to the boatpool in Bowring Park last summer.

To prevent traffic snarls at Rawlins Cross, one of the heaviest congested areas in the city, several policemen were doing special duty in case their services were required.

On the whole, motor cars and trucks were going slower than usual early this morning, but as the day wore on the novelty wore off, engines were being fed more gas and the tempo of driving was quickening.

One of the underlying reasons for the change in the driving rule was the expected merger of the city bus and street car transportation systems, which will be succeeded by electricity-driven trolley buses. It is desirable for passengers to disembark from a bus directly on the sidewalk instead of in the path of traffic, and the only trolley buses obtainable are those from the States and Canada where drive right is the law.

The Evening Telegram
January 2, 1947

Street car No. 14 at Rawlins Cross. Note the policeman in the kiosk controlling the traffic light in the centre of the road. The rule of the road was changed from driving on the left, to driving on the right, on January 2, 1947. The Newfoundland Light & Power park commemorating the first public use of electricity in Newfoundland is located where the house is on the right.

Farewell my sweet

The street cars will make their last run today—Farewell, My Sweet.

For upwards of forty-eight years you have provided a service, faithful and dependable, in sunshine and rain and in snow, a service which, while it may be equalled will surely never be surpassed.

You have seen the weatherman in all his moods, and have proved a happy haven for the hundreds of thousands of grateful pedestrians to whom this change, wrought by the march of time, will bring pangs of bitter regret.

Like that of the City you served so long and diligently, your tempo has kept pace with the time, matching stride for stride the ways of progress, or so 'tis called.

But will, or can, your successor follow in your rumbling trail, keeping bright the record established by your metal heart for lo these four dozen years?

One wonders and remembers at the same time the various works of mercy which you dispensed with an impartiality to be admired.

And recalls his first sight of the mechanical monsters as they appeared in our ancient seaport town at the turn of the century;

Bringing back nostalgic memories of your measured progress through the streets on inaugural day.

And reflection on childhood days when the biggest treat a boy or a girl of six or eight or ten could get was an afternoon spent in riding over the route on a Sunday afternoon, just for the ride.

In years to come it will be just a memory, but who of all your courteous conductors will be able to forget the moppets climbing shyly into the street car.

'Two of us for five cents, mister?'

The answer was always yes.

The good housewife, her arms piled high with packages, likely grasping a tiny tot by the hand—the hundreds of workers daily on their way to the factories, wharves and shops and offices—children going to school—and the mad dash to catch the last car at night when you became older, remember?

These are but a few of the things that a nickel bought in what, after today, will be longingly recalled as the good old days!

Farewell my Sweet!

The Evening Telegram
September 15, 1948

NOTICE!

To Street Car Patrons

The Newfoundland Light and Power Company wish to announce the discontinuance of the Tramway System Operation in the City of St. John's as of Wednesday, this week.

Shortly after noon, that is after the closing of offices and shops, on Wednesday, September 15th, each tramcar as it completes its run to the crossroads at Water Street West will return to the car barn. Buses will then be on hand to continue the Transportation Service.

While many will view the passing of the Tramcar Service with some nostalgic feeling, it must be realized that in order to give a comprehensive Transportation Service to the City, a unified city-wide system is imperative. We feel sure, after a very short while, the people will become accustomed to the new system.

We wish to publicly thank our Street Car Operators for their faithful service. We believe they gave friendly, courteous and efficient service consistently and at times under very trying conditions, both to the patrons of the trams and the operators of other vehicles. Our accident record is something of which to be proud. This despite the number of years of blackout which prevailed during the war.

Most of the Operators will carry on their service to the Public under the sponsorship of the Golden Arrow Coaches Limited. We know they will do their utmost to continue serving you in the best way possible.

Unused street car tickets may be redeemed at either of the Company's Cash Offices.

We wish also to thank our many patrons, who, through the years have been friendly, considerate and cheerful. And so farewell.

Newfoundland
LIGHT & POWER
COMPANY LIMITED
STREET RAILWAY DEPARTMENT

sep14,15,rop   OKA

The Daily News
September 14, 1948

For sale

With the exception of the sweeper, the bodies of all the street cars were recently sold to Mr. Geoffrey Stirling.

Some of these have, it is understood, been disposed of through another party.

The motors and tracks may be utilized by Light and Power Company or sold for scrap if found unsuitable for use.

The Daily News
October 13, 1948

The Daily News
October 4, 1948

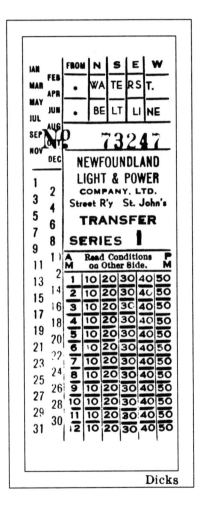

Francis Rowe